MEDITERRANEAN SEA

Jen Green

WORLD ALMANAC® LIBRARY

Please visit our web site at: www.worldalmanaclibrary.com
For a free color catalog describing World Almanac® Library's list of
high-quality books and multimedia programs, call 1-800-848-2928 (USA)
or 1-800-387-3178 (Canada). World Almanac® Library's fax: (414) 332-3567.

Library of Congress Cataloging-in-Publication Data

Green, Jen.
    Mediterranean Sea / Jen Green.
        p. cm. — (Oceans and seas)
    Includes bibliographical references and index.
    ISBN 0-8368-6274-0 (lib. bdg.)
    ISBN 0-8368-6282-1 (softcover)
        1. Mediterranean Sea—Juvenile literature. 1. Title.
    GC651.G74   2006
    551.46'138—dc22   2005052936

First published in 2006 by
World Almanac® Library
A Member of the WRC Media Family of Companies
330 West Olive Street, Suite 100
Milwaukee, WI 53212 USA

Copyright © 2006 by World Almanac® Library.

Produced by Discovery Books
Editor: Sabrina Crewe
Designer and page production: Sabine Beaupré
Photo researcher: Sabrina Crewe
Maps and diagrams: Stefan Chabluk
Geographical consultant: Keith Lye
World Almanac® Library editorial direction: Valerie Weber
World Almanac® Library editor: Gini Holland
World Almanac® Library art direction: Tammy West
World Almanac® Library graphic design: Charlie Dahl
World Almanac® Library production: Jessica Morris and Robert Kraus

Picture credits: Chris Fairclough Worldwide: pp. 25, 39; Corbis: pp. 17, 23, 28, 38, 40;
FLPA: pp. 8, 11, 16, 18–19, 21 (bottom), 22 (both), 27, 29, 34–35, 41; Getty Images: cover,
pp. 4, 10, 12, 15, 26, 32, 36, 42; NOAA: pp. 13 (both), 21 (top), 24, 37 (both); NOAA/
NGDC: title page; NOAA/National Undersea Research Program: p. 31.

Printed in the United States of America

1 2 3 4 5 6 7 8 9 10 09 08 07 06

CONTENTS

Front cover: *Sailing boats sit in the bay at Lindos on the Greek island of Rhodes in the Mediterranean Sea. The white buildings of the town nestle on the hillside below the Acropolis, which was a fortified area in the time of ancient Greece.* Title page: *This computer-generated image of Earth was based on land and ocean measurements made by the U.S. National Geophysical Data Center. This view shows the Mediterranean Sea as the light blue area in the center and slightly to the right, above the continent of Africa.*

Words that appear in the glossary are printed in **boldface** the first time they occur in text.

The Mediterranean is famous for its clear, blue waters, seen here on the Costa Smeralda in Sardinia, Italy.

The Mediterranean Sea, the world's largest inland sea, is a part of the Atlantic Ocean. The sea stretches more than 2,000 miles (3,200 kilometers) from west to east and an average of 500 miles (800 km) from north to south. Many of the world's ancient **civilizations** grew up near the shores of the Mediterranean, including those of the Egyptians, Greeks, and Romans. In ancient times, the sea was the center of the known world for the peoples on its borders. Its name, in fact, means "middle of the land" in Latin.

Boundaries of the Mediterranean

The Mediterranean is almost landlocked, or enclosed, by the continents of Europe to the north, Africa to the south, and Asia to the east. To the west, the **Strait** of Gibraltar, just 8 miles (13 km) across at its narrowest point, leads to the rest of the Atlantic Ocean. Two further channels link the Mediterranean to other bodies of water. In the northeast, the Sea of Marmara and the Bosporus Strait lead to the Black Sea. In the southeast, the Suez

Reason to Travel

"The grand object of traveling is to see the shores of the Mediterranean."

British writer Samuel Johnson (1709–1784)

Canal links the Mediterranean with the Red Sea across the **isthmus** of Suez.

The Mediterranean has many islands, of which Sicily, Sardinia, and Cyprus are the largest. The long **peninsulas** of Italy and Greece extend into the sea. Islands and peninsulas separate the Mediterranean into several smaller seas, including the Tyrrhenian Sea, the Adriatic Sea, the Aegean Sea, and the Ionian Sea.

Resources

The Mediterranean is a sea with many resources. It has provided food for coastal peoples since prehistoric times, and it has been important for shipping and trade for several thousand years. Many ports and cities stand on its shores, and the northern coast in particular is heavily industrialized. The region has long been popular with tourists, who come to enjoy the sunny climate, view ancient ruins, and sample local cultures.

This map shows the Mediterranean Sea, its major islands and underwater features, and the landmasses that border it.

PHYSICAL FEATURES

The salty waters of the Mediterranean Sea occupy a deep basin extending from the Strait of Gibraltar in the west to the shores of Syria, Lebanon, and Israel in the east. The floor of that basin, however, is far from even. The Mediterranean has rugged features, such as long undersea **ridges**, deep trenches, and the tall, cone-shaped peaks named **seamounts**. These undersea landscapes have formed as a result of the slow but continual shifting of the giant slabs of rock, known as tectonic plates, which form Earth's outer layers. These movements and other factors ensure that the Mediterranean Sea is still changing today.

Complex Plates

Beneath the Mediterranean, there are parts of two large plates—the African and Eurasian—and several smaller ones, including the Ionian and Aegean plates. Underneath the seabed, these plates drift and push against one another with enormous force. The tremendous pressure of these plate collisions causes frequent earthquakes and volcanic eruptions in the region. The coasts of Turkey, Greece,

and southern Italy are particularly prone to eruptions and violent quakes.

The ridges, trenches, and some islands of the Mediterranean were shaped by plate movements that took place tens of millions of years ago. Scientists, however, do not agree exactly when the sea formed. Some scientists believe the Mediterranean Sea is a leftover fragment of the ancient Tethys Sea, which formed about 200 million years ago. Others believe the Mediterranean was formed much later, about 44 million years ago.

Samples taken from the floor of the Mediterranean in 1970, by the drilling ship *Glomar Challenger*, appear to support this second theory. **Sediments** from the floor of the Balearic Basin in the west are 25 million years old, while samples from the eastern basin are 70 million years old. Nowhere, however, have sediments been found that date back to the time of the Tethys Sea.

More Plate Movements

There is closer agreement among scientists about dramatic events that took place in the Mediterranean about

Plates and Oceans

Earth's outer layers are made up of a number of vast, rigid sections called tectonic plates—seven major ones and up to twelve smaller ones. Fitting together like pieces of a jigsaw puzzle, the plates underlie oceans and dry land. The plates drift across Earth's surface, floating on a lower, molten layer of the **mantle** like chunks of bread on a thick, bubbling soup. As they drift, tectonic plates can push together, grind past one another, or pull apart.

Volcanic eruptions and earthquakes are common along plate boundaries because the crust is thinnest there. Where two plates pull apart, **magma** rises to fill the space, creating a mountain chain underwater or on land, such as the Alps and the Pyrenees in the northern Mediterranean. Along the border of the Ionian and Aegean plates, a plate collision caused one plate to dive below the other to form a deep trench.

About 250 million years ago, Earth's landmasses were united in a single "super-continent" named Pangaea, which was surrounded by a vast ocean now known as Panthalassa. About 200 million years ago, because of **continental drift** caused by plate movement, a great bay—the Tethys Sea—opened up in the center of Pangaea and split it in half. The northern landmass—named Laurasia—included North America, Greenland, Europe, and Asia, while the southern half—Gondwanaland—included South America, Africa, India, Australia, and Antarctica. As plate movement continued over millions of years, the continents and oceans took their present positions (shown below, with the major tectonic plates), and they continue to shift today.

6 million years ago. About this time, plate movements caused the Strait of Gibraltar to close completely. With no water flowing through the strait, the sea began to dry out. The **evaporation** left behind a thick layer of salt on the dry bed, while shallow, salty lakes remained in the deepest areas. Rivers, including the Rhône and the Nile, cut deep canyons as they plunged down onto the dry bed.

Later—5.4 million years ago—plate movements forced the Strait of Gibraltar to open again. The waters of the Atlantic

A view across the Strait of Gibraltar shows a wide passage of water. Several million years ago, however, this gateway to the Mediterranean closed, and the sea dried up.

cascaded back into the Mediterranean basin in a giant waterfall that refilled the sea in about one hundred years. Many scientists believe this process of drying out and refilling actually happened up to twelve times between 7.5 and 5 million years ago. Huge quantities of **minerals**, known as **evaporites**, were found on the bed of the Mediterranean, and they support this theory. These minerals only form when large amounts of saltwater evaporate.

Features of the Seafloor

At the western end of the Mediterranean, the Strait of Gibraltar is on average 1,000 feet (305 m) deep. It forms a shallow lip between the Mediterranean and the rest of the Atlantic Ocean. Coastal waters all around the sea are shallow, too, because of its continental shelves—these are ledges extending out from the land where the waters are rarely more than 500 feet (152 m) deep. The continental shelves of the Mediterranean are fairly narrow compared to those of the world's open oceans—less than 15 miles (24 km) wide in many places.

A high undersea ridge crosses the Mediterranean between Tunisia in North Africa and Sicily, off southern Italy. The ridge creates an area of shallow water and divides the sea into two main basins. The bed of the Balearic Basin in the west of

the sea is relatively smooth. It is made up of three smaller basins: the Alborán, Algerian, and Tyrrhenian Basins. The floor of the Tyrrhenian Sea, west of Italy, contains soaring seamounts and a deep trough that drops to 12,000 feet (3,650 m). The eastern basin—made up of the Ionian and Levantine Basins—is even more uneven, with several undersea ridges and islands that separate it into smaller areas. The deepest point in the Mediterranean, the Hellenic Trough, lies in the Ionian Basin west of Greece.

Coasts

The coastline of the Mediterranean Sea runs for 28,500 miles (46,000 km) and includes parts of some twenty nations. In the north, the coast of southern Europe is deeply indented, with the large peninsulas of Greece and Italy jutting far out to sea. Where hills and mountain ranges, such as the Alps and Pyrenees, fall steeply to the shore, they create rugged features, including sheer cliffs,

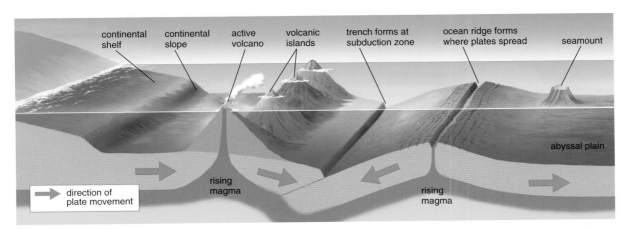

This diagram shows many of the features found on Earth's ocean floors.

rocky **promontories**, and deep bays. In the south, the African coastline is much smoother, with fewer bays and promontories. In Libya and Egypt, the land slopes gently seaward in a broad coastal plain. Where large rivers—the Nile in Egypt, the Rhône in France, and the Po in Italy—join the Mediterranean, they drop sand and sediment to create fan-shaped **deltas** of low-lying, marshy land.

In the last few million years, tectonic plate movements have forced some coasts, including the eastern coast of Italy, to move upward. This creates features such as raised beaches, which now stand high and dry above the sea. Elsewhere, on the Dalmatian coast of Croatia and in northern Sardinia, plate movements have caused the land to sink downward. This sinking can result in features such as drowned river **estuaries** and islands that were once hills on the mainland. The islands parallel to the Dalmatian coast in the Adriatic Sea were formed in this way.

An aerial view of the Nile Delta in Egypt clearly shows the fan-shaped area of marshland at the river mouth. The delta of the Nile is huge, covering 19,500 square miles (50,500 sq km).

For the past few hundred years, other changes, made by people, have altered many parts of the Mediterranean coastline. Sea walls built to protect one stretch of coast from erosion, for example, often increase the rate of erosion on neighboring shorelines by diverting waves in their direction. Rivers have been dammed, which affects the flow of water reaching the Mediterranean. The 1970 opening of the Aswan High Dam in Egypt greatly reduced the flow of water from the Nile River. This reduction, among other factors, is eroding the Nile Delta.

Many Islands

The Mediterranean is famous for its many islands. The largest, Sicily, covers more than 9,800 square miles (25,400 sq km).

Shaping Coastlines

The coastal landscapes of the Mediterranean are shaped by two main processes: erosion and deposition. Erosion is the wearing away of the land by water, wind, and other natural forces. Deposition is the laying down of rocky materials, or deposits, often in the form of fine particles such as sand, mud, or silt.

Waves are the main force of erosion on coastlines. As they beat against the shore, they hurl sand and **shingle** against rocks to wear them away. Bands of hard rock at the water's edge are left to form jutting headlands, while soft rocks are eaten away to form deep, curving bays. In some parts of the Mediterranean, waves are eating into coasts by 3 feet (1 m) or more each year, gradually shifting the shore inland. Around the delta of the Po River in Italy, the land is sinking, which is increasing the rate of coastal erosion. High tides often flood the city of Venice, which is built on a group of small, sinking islands in a coastal lagoon.

Out to sea, the pounding waves smash rocky fragments into sand and shingle. Coastal **currents** may carry these materials for miles along the shore and then deposit them to form offshore **spits** and the fine sandy beaches for which the Mediterranean is renowned.

Rocky headlands and bays are features of the Mediterranean coastline that were created by erosion. Beaches, such as the one in this bay on the island of Sardinia, are created by deposition.

The Cyclades Islands in the Aegean Sea east of Greece are among many groups of small islands found in the Mediterranean Sea.

The islands of the Mediterranean have several different origins. Sardinia, Corsica, and Sicily were once part of mainland Africa and Europe and are known as continental islands. Millions of years ago, continental drift caused these fragments to break away from mainlands and gradually shift into their present positions. Other islands were part of the mainland as recently as twenty thousand years ago, during the last ice age. At that time, Earth's climate was colder than it is today, and ice covered much of the northern hemisphere. Sea levels were lower because so much moisture was locked up as ice. Later, as the climate

Sardinia and Corsica to the west of Italy, and Crete and Cyprus in the east, are also sizeable islands. The eastern basin holds thousands of smaller islands often found in clusters, such as the Cyclades and Dodecanese groups in the Aegean.

Vesuvius

One of the most famous volcanoes on the Mediterranean coast is Mount Vesuvius, on the Bay of Naples in Italy. It has erupted numerous times, causing great devastation. After several hundred quiet years, Vesuvius erupted in A.D. 79, destroying the Roman cities of Herculaneum and Pompeii. A column of ash, perhaps 20 miles (32 km) high, rose from the volcano, and the surrounding areas were showered with burning cinders, ash, and rock. A 10-foot (3-m) layer of volcanic rock and ash fell on Pompeii; Herculaneum, closer to the volcano, was buried under 75 feet (23 m). Most of the ten thousand people in the area who died were suffocated by volcanic gases. Many bodies were buried by ash.

Vesuvius is still an active volcano. It has erupted numerous times since A.D. 79. The last time was in 1944, but it is still regarded as one of the world's most dangerous volcanoes. More than two million people live on the slopes of Vesuvius and in the immediate surrounding area.

Mount Etna, Sicily, is shown during one of its frequent eruptions. The satellite image (inset), made by the U.S. National Climactic Data Center, shows the plume of smoke and ash from a 2001 eruption blowing across the Mediterranean Sea.

warmed, the ice melted and sea levels rose, flooding coastal regions. Hills near the coast were cut off by the sea to become islands.

Volcanoes and Volcanic Islands

Yet other islands are volcanic in origin. In the Mediterranean, volcanic islands have formed close to **subduction zones**, where two plates collide on the sea floor and one is forced to dive below the other. An example is the border between the Ionian and Aegean plates. Rock that has been forced downward melted and surged up again to form volcanic islands, including Santorini (or Thíra) in the Cyclades Islands.

About 1650–1645 B.C., Santorini was torn apart by a huge eruption. Gases that had built up in the hollow chamber below the volcano caused the massive explosion. The whole top of the island was blown away, leaving just a ring of land around a central crater that filled with seawater. Huge amounts of dust were dispersed into the atmosphere over the whole Mediterranean region.

Mount Etna on the island of Sicily is Europe's highest active volcano, rising to about 10,960 feet (3,340 m). Its central cone, which has changed shape over years of eruptions, is pitted with more than 250 craters from smaller eruptions in its sides. Etna continues to erupt frequently.

CHAPTER TWO

CLIMATE AND CURRENTS

Saltwater enters the Mediterranean from the wider Atlantic Ocean and from the Black Sea. Rivers such as the Rhône, Po, Nile, and the Ebro in Spain add freshwater. The dry, sunny climate of the Mediterranean causes huge amounts of water to evaporate from the sea surface, especially in summer. Each year, large quantities of water are lost from the Mediterranean as the Sun heats the water surface. The Mediterranean, in fact, loses three times as much water through evaporation as it gains from rainfall and rivers. The shortfall is made up by seawater flowing from the wider Atlantic Ocean through the Strait of Gibraltar.

The Water Cycle

Moisture continually circulates between the oceans, air, and land. This never-ending process, called the water cycle, is illustrated here. The Sun beating down on the ocean surface causes moisture to rise into the air in the form of a gas, water vapor. This process of turning liquid into gas is called evaporation. As the warm, moist air rises, it cools. Cold air can hold less moisture than warm air, and so the moisture in it **condenses** to form clouds, which may drift over the land before shedding rain. When rain falls on land, any moisture not absorbed by plants or soil drains away into streams and rivers. The water then runs into the ocean to begin the cycle again.

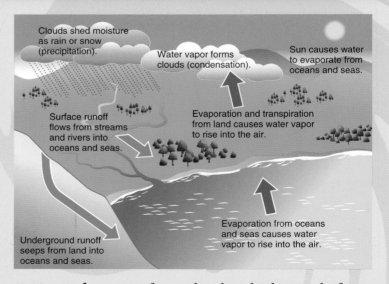

Clouds shed moisture as rain or snow (precipitation).

Water vapor forms clouds (condensation).

Sun causes water to evaporate from oceans and seas.

Surface runoff flows from streams and rivers into oceans and seas.

Evaporation and transpiration from land causes water vapor to rise into the air.

Underground runoff seeps from land into oceans and seas.

Evaporation from oceans and seas causes water vapor to rise into the air.

Salty Waters

The waters of the Mediterranean are saltier than the rest of the Atlantic because of its high levels of evaporation, which concentrate salt in the upper waters. The average **salinity** of the oceans is about 34 parts per 1,000. The Mediterranean is saltier, with more than 36 parts of salt per 1,000, rising to nearly 40 parts in the eastern basin where the hot, dry climate causes most evaporation. The far western end is less salty because of the inflow of water from the wider Atlantic.

Currents

This inflow forms a surface current that travels from the Strait of Gibraltar south and east along the North African coast. The current creates a counterclockwise

Why Is the Sea Salty?

Seawater is salty because it contains dissolved minerals, or salts, washed from the land by rivers or released underwater from **hydrothermal vents** and volcanic eruptions. The salt level in seawater is higher than in rivers because, when surface water evaporates, the dissolved salts remain in the sea and become more concentrated. Experts calculate that the salt in all the seas and oceans would be enough to bury Earth's landmasses to a depth of 500 feet (152 m)! So why don't seas get increasingly salty as new minerals are added each year? Some salt is removed from the water when it is absorbed by marine life or reacts with underwater rock and eventually forms new sediment layers on the ocean floor. These processes help keep salt levels constant in seas and oceans.

gyre that is the main surface current in the Mediterranean, flowing right around the coasts to return to Gibraltar. Scientists estimate that Mediterranean water takes about 150 years to complete

Saltwater is more buoyant than freshwater, which makes the Mediterranean Sea very pleasant for swimmers, who can float easily in its salty surface waters.

this circuit. In winter, the surface water cools, sinks, and eventually leaves the Mediterranean as a deepwater current passing through the Strait of Gibraltar.

A Warm Climate

The average temperature of surface waters in the Mediterranean is 60° Fahrenheit (16° Celsius). Surface temperatures rise to 86° F (30° C) in summer off the Libyan coast, while in winter they may fall to 41° F (5° C) in the Adriatic. The temperature of bottom waters is more constant, always remaining between 53° F and 59° F (12° C and 15° C).

The warmth of the Mediterranean Sea influences the climate of surrounding regions. Most coastal areas experience hot, dry summers, while winters in the north are mild and rainy. The climate favors the growth of grapevines and many kinds of fruit trees in coastal areas, while grain crops thrive in irrigated fields. The North African coast, which is closer to the equator, has a hotter and drier climate, with less rainfall.

Winds and Waves

Mountains around the Mediterranean Sea shelter it from winds on many sides, but some pass through gaps in the mountains or sweep over coastal plains. A hot, dry wind—named the Sirocco—blows north from the Sahara Desert in Africa toward Europe. A dry, cold wind—the Mistral—blows in the opposite direction, south from France toward Africa. The strongest winds occur in winter, when dull, wet weather blows in from the wider Atlantic Ocean.

Olive trees thrive in the dry, sunny climate of coastal hillsides in Greece and other Mediterranean nations. Greek olives and olive oil are consumed all over the world.

The waves of the Mediterranean are generally smaller than in open oceans because of the relatively light winds and enclosed nature of the region. Winter **squalls** from the wider Atlantic can ruffle the Mediterranean's surface into large waves, however, which smash onto coasts. Tsunamis are rare, but not unknown, in the Mediterranean. These huge, freak waves can form when earthquakes, volcanic eruptions, or landslides disturb the seabed. The towering waves radiate out from the center of disturbance like ripples from a pebble tossed into a pond.

This cruise ship carrying over seven hundred passengers was rocked by huge waves in the Mediterranean Sea. The ship lost its communications system and electrical power while the storm raged.

What Causes Tides?

Tides are regular rises and falls in sea level caused mainly by the tug of the Moon's gravity. As the Moon orbits Earth, its gravity pulls ocean water into a mound below it. A similar bulge appears on the ocean on the opposite side of Earth because the planet itself is also being pulled, by the same force, away from the water on the far side. As Earth spins eastward, so the mounds move westward across Earth's surface, bringing tides to coasts in succession. Because Earth spins around once every twenty-four hours, the two bulges both move across Earth once in that period, creating two tides a day in each place.

The Sun's gravity exerts a similar, but weaker, pull on the oceans. This is because, while many times larger than the Moon, it is also much farther away. Every two weeks, at the full moon and again during the new moon, the Sun and Moon line up so that their pulls combine. This force brings extra-high tides called spring tides. They alternate with weaker tides also occurring every two weeks, named neap tides, when the two pulls tend to minimize each other.

The Mediterranean Sea is renowned for its slight tides. On many coasts, tides are barely noticeable, with the water level varying by only about 1 foot (0.3 m). The maximum tidal range (the difference between high and low water) in the region is about 3 feet (1 m).

CHAPTER THREE

MARINE LIFE

The Mediterranean Sea is home to more than twelve thousand identified species of plants and animals, of which about one-third are found nowhere else in the world. Thousands more species are thought to exist there but have not yet been identified. Most plants and animals of the Mediterranean are related to those in the rest of the Atlantic. They entered long ago with the water flowing through the Strait of Gibraltar and then gradually adapted to suit the particular conditions found in this warm, sheltered sea.

Coastal Habitats

The waters, coasts, and islands of the Mediterranean offer a variety of **habitats** to suit different species. Coastal habitats include **lagoons**, mudflats, and reed beds. Crabs, worms, and **mollusks** burrow in the sand or mud of beaches, while anemones, fish, and starfish inhabit pools on rocky shores. Marshlands,

including the Coto Doñana in Spain, act as nurseries for millions of young birds, fish, and shellfish. Flamingos and wild horses inhabit the marshy delta of the Camargue in southern France, where the Rhône River reaches the sea.

Open Water

Farther out to sea, different species thrive at various depths in the water. The warm, sunlit surface waters, or **euphotic zone**, support seaweed and floating **plankton**, which feed shrimp, jellyfish, and surface-dwelling fish such as anchovy and mackerel. Blue sharks and squid swim in the mid-depths, or **bathyal zone**.

Flamingos wade in shallow water in the Camargue, France. These long-legged birds feed by holding their heads upside down in the water and filtering food with their sieve-like beaks. The pink tint of these birds' plumage comes from the shrimp they eat.

The upper waters of the bathyal zone are sometimes called the "twilight zone" because glimmers of sunlight brighten the gloom there. Some squid and fish in the twilight zone have light-producing organs, called photophores, on their undersides. These organs give off gleams of light that help fish and squid blend in with the sunlight above, making them less visible to other marine animals below.

In the black depths of the **abyssal zone**, below 6,600 feet (2,000 m), sea creatures feed on the remains of dead plants and animals that fall down from above, or they prey on each other. Relatively few species, however, inhabit the deep waters of the Mediterranean because not many deep-sea species have managed to cross from the Atlantic Ocean through the shallow Strait of Gibraltar. Sperm whales are among the few large creatures that visit the abyss. These mammals take in gulps of air at the surface, and then they plunge to the depths to hunt their favorite prey— the deep-sea squid.

Plants

Plant life of the Mediterranean includes many types of seaweed. Red seaweeds, which flourish in warm water, are more common here than the brown varieties that prefer cooler seas. Sea grasses thrive in coastal shallows because the slight tides of the Mediterranean allow the nearly constant level of the sea to keep the plants submerged. These grasses trap drifting sediment, and they feed creatures such as shrimp, pipefish, and turtles.

Microscopic plankton drift at the surface, providing food for marine life of all kinds. Plankton is less abundant here than in the rest of the Atlantic Ocean or in the Black Sea because of the scarcity of nutrients. Nutrients are limited because less cold, nutrient-rich water wells up from the depths, and there are relatively few rivers bringing nutrients

Ocean Food Chains

In the Mediterranean Sea, living things depend on one another for food. The relationships between plants and animals in a habitat can be shown in a food chain. Plants form the base of almost all marine food chains. Seaweeds and microscopic floating plants, or phytoplankton, use light to make their food, through the process of **photosynthesis**. Tiny animals called zooplankton, including young fish and shellfish, feed on plant plankton. They in turn provide food for small fish, such as anchovies, which may be eaten by larger fish—mackerel, for example. Seals, dolphins, and large fish, including swordfish and sharks, are powerful predators at the top of the Mediterranean food chain. When these animals and other living things die, their remains are eaten by scavenging shrimps, crabs, and microbes, which helps to recycle the energy their bodies contain.

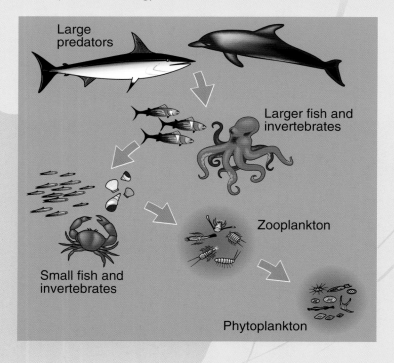

Large predators

Larger fish and invertebrates

Small fish and invertebrates

Zooplankton

Phytoplankton

into the sea. This scarcity limits the abundance of life found in deeper Mediterranean waters.

Invertebrates

Most animals found in the Mediterranean Sea are invertebrates—creatures such as mollusks, shellfish, jellyfish, and sponges that lack a bony inner skeleton. Sponges, sea anemones, starfish, snails, and sea urchins live on the sea bottom. They are either permanently anchored there or move about relatively little. Many of these species feed by taking in seawater and filtering out and consuming the small creatures floating in it. One such creature is the murex, a type of sea snail found in the Mediterranean. It was prized in ancient times because it produced a bright dye that was used to stain emperors' robes deep purple. Squid and octopus are mollusks like the murex, but they are free-swimming creatures. Both can squirt a jet of water—through a tubelike siphon

These huge tuna (above) were photographed off the Italian island of Sicily. A group of Mediterranean fairy basslet (right) swims over colorful corals near the coast of Spain.

near their heads—to escape their enemies with a sudden burst of speed.

Mediterranean invertebrates also include several types of stinging or spiny creatures that can harm humans. A jellyfish named the sea wasp can deliver a painful sting with its long, trailing tentacles. Black, spiky sea urchins that inhabit the shallow waters of the Mediterranean use their sharp spines to injure unwary swimmers and waders that step on them.

Fish and Reptiles

Over five hundred species of fish live in the Mediterranean, ranging in size from tiny anchovies to massive tuna. Biologists divide them into pelagic species, which are surface dwellers, and demersal (bottom-dwelling) fish. Flying fish, sardines, and anchovies are among the

fish that swim in groups, or schools, at the surface. Flying fish can leap right out of the water and glide for several yards on their winglike fins to escape predators such as tuna. Bottom dwellers, which include plaice, sole, skate, and rays, have flattened bodies that help them swim along the seabed. Pipefish have long, slim bodies that disguise them among the waving blades of sea grass, where they swim with an upright posture. Swordfish and tuna arrive from other parts of the Atlantic Ocean at certain times of year.

Marine reptiles include green turtles that live at sea but scramble ashore to lay their eggs on beaches in Greece and Turkey. Loggerhead turtles, which swim

Migrating Birds

Many species of land birds visit the Mediterranean in spring and fall, as they move between their summer breeding grounds in Europe or Asia and their winter habitats in Africa. These seasonal journeys are known as **migrations**. Crossing the open sea is dangerous. Birds keep to their regular migration routes, or flyways, which cross the sea at its narrowest points, the Strait of Gibraltar and the shallows between Sicily and Tunisia. They also fly along the Mediterranean's eastern edge. Small songbirds, such as swallows and martins, migrate mostly at night, while larger birds, such as storks, buzzards, and eagles, usually cross the sea by day.

A Barbary ape (below) sits on the seawall overlooking the Strait of Gibraltar. A Mediterranean monk seal (below right) swims near the coast of Greece.

in from the wider Atlantic, are among the biggest turtles in the oceans, weighing on average 300 pounds (136 kilograms).

Birds of the Mediterranean

Fewer seabirds are found in the waters of the Mediterranean than in more northern waters because fish are less abundant here. Birds of open waters include gulls, terns, and shearwaters. Wading birds are seen on coasts, particularly in winter, when they fly in to escape harsher conditions farther north. Cory's shearwater and Audouin's gull are among bird species found only in the Mediterranean.

Mediterranean Mammals

Among mammals, the Mediterranean monk seal is the only member of the seal family found in these waters. One of the largest seals, weighing anywhere from 530 to 880 pounds (240 to 400 kg), the monk seal is also one of the rarest. Only a few hundred of these animals are thought to survive, breeding in rocky coves on remote coasts. A type of monkey, the Barbary ape, lives on the

Rock of Gibraltar off the coast of southern Spain. Its presence there is a mystery. Some experts think the monkeys were originally brought from North Africa by the Romans.

Nineteen species of whales are known to live in or visit the Mediterranean. Baleen whales, such as fin and minke whales, filter shrimp and fish from the water, using the comblike plates of baleen hanging down inside their mouths. Toothed whales include sperm whales, orcas, and several types of porpoise and dolphin.

Dolphins have an exceptional relationship with people. In the Turkish city of Antalya on the Mediterranean coast, dolphins are used in therapy sessions (above) for children who suffer from cerebral palsy.

Dolphins are highly intelligent mammals that live in groups, or schools. They find their prey by **echolocation**. The dolphins produce streams of clicking sounds and listen for echoes bouncing back off schools of fish. These naturally sociable animals have been known to help swimmers in trouble, and they are often seen swimming alongside boats.

CHAPTER FOUR

PEOPLE AND SETTLEMENT

The mild climate of the Mediterranean Sea and its coasts has favored habitation since prehistoric times. The sea offered food in the form of fish and shellfish. After people learned how to build boats, the sea offered a means of transportation.

Early Humans

Scientific study indicates that modern humans inhabited some coasts of the Mediterranean as far back as 100,000 years ago. People have also inhabited islands in the Mediterranean since prehistoric times.

Western Civilization

The Mediterranean is often called the "cradle of western civilization." About 10,000 years ago, people began farming and keeping herds of sheep and goats in an area named the Fertile Crescent, which stretched from the eastern part of the Mediterranean to the Persian Gulf. This is thought to be the first example of farming anywhere in the world. Some of the world's first towns grew up in the eastern Mediterranean about 8000 B.C.—at Jericho in the ancient land of Palestine, for example, and at Catal Huyuk in southern Turkey. By 3,500 years ago, the people of this region had discovered how to **forge** bronze to make tools and weapons that were stronger than the stone tools used previously.

Development of Many Cultures

Beginning in about 4000 B.C., the region around the Mediterranean was

People have fished in Mediterranean waters for thousands of years. This rock painting, showing dolphins and fish among other images, is in the Grotto del Genovese on the Italian island of Levanso. The painting is about six thousand years old.

The world's first agriculture probably took place on the shores of the Mediterranean. Many peoples of the region grow grapes in vineyards like this one in coastal France.

home to some of the world's advanced ancient cultures. One of the first was that of the Egyptians, which developed on the banks of the Nile River. The Egyptians were skilled farmers who drew water from the river to irrigate their fields. They also built the largest structures in the ancient world— the Pyramids— and devised an early form of writing. The Egyptians established a powerful civilization.

About 3000 B.C., the sea-based Minoan culture flourished on the island of Crete. In the period 1650–1645 B.C., however, the eruption of the Greek island of Santorini to the north sent tsunamis racing across the water. Waves wrecked the cities of the Minoan civilization on Crete and probably hastened the end of the culture by 1100 B.C. This event may have given rise to the legend of Atlantis—the tale of a beautiful island city that was mysteriously swamped by waves and swallowed up by the sea.

Beginning in about 2000 B.C., the Greek civilization thrived in mainland Greece. Greek city states sprang up around the shores of the Aegean, "like frogs around a pond," in the words of one Greek writer. The ancient Greeks are known as great philosophers and

mathematicians. The philosopher Aristotle is credited with founding the science of **oceanography** in the 300s B.C. The Greeks also came up with the political system of democracy—the word *politics*, in fact, comes from *polis*, the Greek word for city. Beautiful temples, theaters, sports stadiums, and whole cities built by the ancient Greeks still stand on coasts of the eastern Mediterranean.

Dispensing Equality

"Democracy . . . is a charming form of government, full of variety and disorder, and dispensing a sort of equality to equals and unequals alike."

Greek philosopher Plato (427–347 B.C.), still considered the most influential philosopher of western civilization

Eyewitness

In A.D. 79, Roman writer Pliny the Younger witnessed the eruption of Mount Vesuvius on the southwestern coast of Italy. The writer, then a young man, watched a huge cloud of ash rise from the volcano's cone, "shaped like a pine tree. Hurled into the air like a great tree trunk, it opened out into branches that rose high in the air through the force of the blast." Pliny's uncle, a scientist, was killed when he approached Pompeii by boat to take a closer look. Pliny escaped inland with his mother.

The ruins of the Roman city of Pompeii, buried by volcanic ash in A.D. 79, still stand in the shadow of Vesuvius.

From 1200 to 500 B.C., another important group, the Phoenicians, dominated parts of the Mediterranean. A civilization of expert seafarers, the Phoenicians opened trade throughout the Mediterranean, transporting goods such as copper from Cyprus, silver from Spain, and tin from Britain. Phoenician **colonies** included Cyprus, southern Spain, and much of North Africa, where Phoenicians founded the mighty city of Carthage in what is now Tunisia.

The Roman Empire

Beginning about 240 B.C., the Roman civilization—based in Rome, Italy—began to spread its influence beyond mainland Italy. By about two hundred years later, the Roman **Empire** dominated the Mediterranean and many other lands from Britain to Palestine. Roman culture and technology spread throughout the Mediterranean, which the Romans named *mare nostrum,* meaning "our sea." While the Romans worshiped their own gods and goddesses, the Christian religion took root in the Roman province of Judea in Palestine in the first century A.D.

In A.D. 324, the emperor Constantine took over the eastern branch of the Roman Empire. Constantine based that branch, now known as the Byzantine Empire, in Byzantium on the Bosporus Strait. The city, which was rebuilt and renamed Constantinople, is now the Turkish capital, Istanbul. The Roman Empire itself declined by A.D. 500.

A twelfth-century fort stands over the harbor at Hammamet in Tunisia, a mostly Muslim nation in North Africa.

Religious Conflict

Beginning in the 600s, Arab Muslims (who followed the religion of Islam) began to take over Mediterranean lands. The mighty Ottoman Empire (c. 1299–1923) of the Muslim Turks included most Mediterranean lands at the height of its powers. The historic culture of the Muslims, as well as those of the ancient Greeks and Romans, live on in the languages, arts, customs, and religions of the many Mediterranean peoples today.

Through the centuries, opposing religious groups—especially Muslims, Christians, and Jews—have fought many wars in the region. In the 1100s and 1200s, Christians fought Muslims for control of Palestine, in a series of wars called the Crusades. The Jewish state of Israel has, more recently, fought several wars with its Arab neighbors in the same region. In the 1990s, religious differences led to war in Bosnia on the eastern Adriatic coast.

Military Importance

Throughout history, Mediterranean coasts and islands have held strategic importance for the people on its borders, particularly in times of war. In the 1900s, battles were fought in the region during both World Wars. The **Cold War**, a time of hostility between western political powers—most notably the United States and the Soviet Union—followed World War II. During this period, the Mediterranean Sea gained new military importance for the United States, western European nations, and the Soviet Union, which had ports on the neighboring Black Sea. Military bases were strengthened on coasts and islands, and submarines and ships patrolled the sea.

The Growth of Ports and Cities

From ancient times, towns and ports grew up in the bays and harbors across the Mediterranean that offered safe mooring for ships. By **medieval** times,

27

The City of Istanbul

The city of Istanbul, once called Byzantium, commands a strategic position along the shores of the Bosporus Strait that leads from the Mediterranean to the Black Sea. In A.D. 324, the emperor Constantine renamed the city Constantinople and made it capital of the Byzantine Empire. In medieval times, it was one of the foremost ports in the Mediterranean, controlling trade between Europe and the Black Sea. Constantinople was captured by Ottoman Turks in 1453 and became part of the Ottoman Empire. Renamed Istanbul, it served as the Ottoman capital for 450 years. For over 2,000 years, the ancient city has been important for industry and other business. Once the capital of Turkey, it is a major destination for tourists. They come to admire historic buildings, such as the church of Hagia Sophia (*center right*) and the mosque of Sultan Ahmed (*front middle*) with their tall, graceful towers.

Constantinople (now Istanbul), Barcelona in Spain, and the Italian ports of Genoa and Venice were all great trading centers, with links to India, China, and Southeast Asia.

In the 1800s, wool, silk, and cotton were the main goods produced by Mediterranean factories. By 1900, industry in the Mediterranean was based in four ports—Barcelona, Istanbul, Marseille in France, and Alexandria in Egypt—and the inland city of Milan, Italy. Today, many other ports, such as Thessaloniki and Piraeus in Greece, Trieste and Naples in Italy, and Haifa and Tel Aviv in Israel, are important manufacturing centers.

Migration to and from the Mediterranean

While the main ports grew wealthy through trade, other settlements around the shores of the Mediterranean remained small. Poor farmers and fishermen scratched a living from the soil or fished from tiny harbors. During the 1800s and early 1900s, war or poverty forced thousands of people to leave coastal villages in Greece and Italy to seek new lives in North America or Australia.

The decades following World War II saw another migration, this time to the eastern Mediterranean. Jewish people from all over the world arrived to settle the new state of Israel, which was formed in 1948 from part of Palestine.

The Mediterranean Today

Today, textiles are still an important Mediterranean industry, but the region is also known for its steel, chemicals, vehicles, wine, and canned foods. Italy, France, and Spain are the leading manufacturing nations. Others include Greece, Turkey, Egypt, and Israel.

Today, the northern coasts of the Mediterranean are heavily populated.

Coastal plains and river valleys, such as the Po and Rhône, have many large industrial towns, while extensive docks and factories have grown up around ports. The coasts of Italy, Spain, Greece, and other countries still have many tiny farming communities and small fishing villages, but some of these are now important for tourism.

In contrast to the heavily developed northern shores of the Mediterranean, the southern and eastern coasts have fewer settlements, with large stretches of mainly barren land on the coast. Even these lands, however, are becoming more populated. Over 40 percent of all people in countries bordering the Mediterranean now live on its coasts, and this figure is rising rapidly. More and more people are moving to coastal areas, especially in Egypt, Algeria, Morocco, and Turkey.

Where the Nile Delta meets the Mediterranean Sea at Alexandria, Egypt, oil refineries are replacing fishing grounds and engulfing wildlife habitats.

CHAPTER FIVE

TRANSPORTATION AND COMMUNICATION

The Mediterranean Sea has been one of the world's busiest waterways for several thousand years. The designs of ships and the cargoes they carry have changed over time. So have **navigation** systems and shipping routes.

Early Vessels

The steady winds, relatively calm waters, and fine natural harbors of the Mediterranean aided early sailors. By 2000 B.C., the Egyptians were sailing coastal waters in reed boats with square sails and a steering oar at the stern (the rear of the boat). The Phoenicians had a similar boat design, but their boats were made of wood and used to transport cargoes of wine, minerals, and nuts across the length of the Mediterranean. The Phoenicians ventured beyond the Strait of Gibraltar to explore the Atlantic coast of West Africa. The Greeks and Romans built two main kinds of ships: warships and cargo vessels. The cargo vessels carried oil, lamps, minerals, produce, and wine around their empires.

Dhows, Caravels, and Carracks

After the fall of the Roman Empire, Arab and Byzantine ships dominated the Mediterranean. By the 700s, Arab sailors were using boats called dhows with triangular sails. The sails enabled them to sail into the wind, which no ships had done before.

In medieval times, Europeans made many advances in boat building. During the 1400s, they combined the best features of Arab and northern European ship designs to build fast, maneuverable vessels called caravels and carracks, which employed both triangular and square sails. In the late 1400s and 1500s, these sturdy wooden vessels were used to cross the world's great oceans and reach faraway lands, including the Americas.

From Steamships to Airplanes

After the mid-1800s, steam began to replace sails as a means of propulsion, and steel **hulls** replaced wooden ones. Modern vessels in the Mediterranean are powered by diesel, gas, or nuclear power. A huge range of vessels now use the busy sea, from large oil **tankers** and **container** ships to cruisers, ferries, yachts, and fishing **trawlers**. Oil and minerals from Africa and the Middle East are transported to Europe, while manufactured goods leave Mediterranean ports for distant lands.

The first airplanes flew over the Mediterranean in the early 1900s, linking cities in Europe, Africa, and Asia. Since the mid-1900s, cheap flights have carried many millions of tourists to coastal resorts in Spain, Greece, and Italy. During the late 1900s, air-craft were increasingly used for business travel and to carry **freight**, including foods that would not survive a long journey by sea.

A sixteenth-century painting shows Alexander the Great being lowered into the Mediterranean in a glass diving bell. Alexander was king of a huge empire that included the Mediterranean region and lands to the east, north, and south.

Submersibles

According to ancient history, Greek conqueror Alexander the Great was one of the first people to view the undersea world. In the 300s B.C., he was lowered to the bed of the Mediterranean in a type of **submersible**, a diving bell fitted with a glass window.

Powered submarines were first used many centuries later, in the 1870s, including in Mediterranean waters. Submarines developed rapidly during

World Wars I and II, when they were used for **reconnaissance** missions and to launch attacks on enemy vessels. Submarines can take advantage of the Mediterranean's deep, westward-moving current to save fuel and help avoid detection as they enter the wider Atlantic. They turn off their engines and glide silently through the Strait of Gibraltar, propelled by the bottom current.

In 1959, French oceanographer and filmmaker Jacques-Yves Cousteau (1910–1997) designed a streamlined submersible named the *soucoupe*, or diving saucer. It was a forerunner to later submersible designs.

Navigating the Mediterranean

The first sailors to navigate the waters of the Mediterranean either kept within sight of land or used their knowledge of wind, waves, and currents to find their way. They measured the position of the midday Sun—and the Moon and stars at night—to work out their **latitude**. The ancient Greeks invented a working model

A lighthouse on Mallorca, one of the Balearic Islands, warns sailors away from dangerous rocks and guides them in coastal waters.

of the heavens, known as an astrolabe. Arab sailors improved this device for navigation, and they also used an instrument called a *kamal* to measure the height of stars and thus determine their location.

By about A.D. 1200, both Arab and European sailors were using magnetic compasses. By the end of that century, Europeans were using detailed charts called *portolans* to navigate across the Mediterranean Sea. European navigators later developed a device, the sextant, to measure the height of the Sun and stars above the horizon and so calculate latitude.

Finding **longitude** was made possible by the invention of a reliable marine chronometer in the 1770s. The chronometer was a clock that helped measure the distance between two places by accurately telling time. The chronometer told sailors the exact time in Greenwich, England, which they compared to their local time to work out their distance east or west of that site, or their longitude.

Modern ships are equipped with a wide range of sensitive instruments that allow them to pinpoint their locations and navigate treacherous waters. These include **sonar** and **radar**, which detects navigation **buoys**. More recently, gyrocompasses and global positioning systems (GPS) have helped ships locate their position using satellites.

Communication Systems

The ancient Greeks were pioneers of marine communication. They used flags or flashing lights to send coded signals from ship to shore. In ancient times, lighthouses and huge statues with lighted beacons were used to guide ships into harbor or warn them away from rocks. Today, ship-to-shore radios allow ships to maintain regular contact with ports and weather stations.

Shipping Routes

The Mediterranean was the world's most important waterway from the time of the Phoenicians through to medieval times. For hundreds of years, silks and spices from India and China traveled overland to the eastern Mediterranean. They were then shipped to the ports of western Europe.

In the late 1400s, Portuguese sailors pioneered a sea route to the East via the Cape of Good Hope at the southern tip

Sonar

In the early 1900s, the development of sonar made it possible for ships to locate underwater hazards and for fishing fleets to find schools of fish. Sonar works with a transmitter that aims pulses of sound waves at the seabed. A receiver then times how long the echoes take to bounce back, and this indicates depth. The first accurate charts of the ocean floor and seafloor were produced using sonar. Detailed maps of the Mediterranean floor are also made using satellites, which give off **microwaves** rather than sound waves.

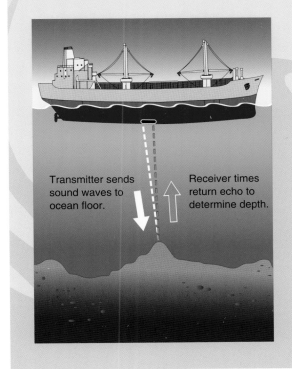

Transmitter sends sound waves to ocean floor.

Receiver times return echo to determine depth.

of Africa. Ships began using this new route, and the volume of shipping in the Mediterranean Sea dropped sharply until 1869, when the Suez Canal between the Mediterranean and Red Sea opened. The new canal created a shortcut between the Atlantic and Indian Oceans. The fast route revived shipping traffic across the Mediterranean, and now more than twenty thousand vessels use this 100-mile (160-km) waterway each year.

The Congested Bosporus

The Bosporus Strait that leads to the Black Sea is one of the world's most congested sea routes. The strait is narrow, dangerous to navigate, and runs through the heart of the ancient Turkish city of Istanbul. Oil tankers coming from Russia and Central Asia carry an estimated three million barrels of oil a day through the strait. As oil production and vessel traffic has increased in the last few years, accidents in the Bosporus Strait have surged. In 2002 and 2003, Turkey introduced safety regulations, but the congestion and threat of a major disaster continue.

Undersea Exploration

Scientific study of the seabed and waters of the Mediterranean dates back to the early 1700s. In 1724, Italian geologist Luigi Ferdinando Marsili (1658–1730) made the first-ever map of the seabed from **soundings** taken off the coast of Marseille in France. Marsili's chart showed the edge of the continental shelf dropping away into deep water. Marsili also studied salt levels, tides, and currents in the Mediterranean Sea.

Several studies took place in the 1940s to 1960s, including those by Jacques Cousteau in his ship *Calypso*. Cousteau also produced a stream of popular books, movies, and television programs that introduced millions of people to the wonders of oceanography. Modern research into the region's climate, the sea's deepwater circulation patterns, and sediments on the seabed are carried out using a variety of sophisticated cameras and scanners carried by satellites, manned and unmanned submersibles, and research and drilling ships.

In 1943, Cousteau and his colleague Emile Gagnan invented scuba-diving equipment that allowed divers to explore the undersea world with an oxygen tank strapped to their backs. Scuba diving soon became a popular pastime.

Marine Archaeology

Over the centuries, many vessels have been lost in Mediterranean waters. The depths contain the wrecks of cargo vessels and warships dating from past centuries, which yield not only precious objects, but important information about everyday life long ago. Following the invention of sonar and scuba-diving equipment, people began to **salvage** valuables from Greek, Roman, Phoenician, and other vessels found in the depths of the Mediterranean. In 1960, a team of divers from the University of Pennsylvania Museum excavated a wreck dating from the 1200s B.C. that had sunk in waters off the Turkish coast.

The remains of buildings that were once on land are also excavated in coastal waters. In 1996, the ruins of the palace of Queen Cleopatra were uncovered in the harbor of Alexandria, Egypt. Marine archaeologists now use unmanned submersibles, sonar, and GPS to make discoveries in the waters of the Mediterranean.

Scuba diving is a favorite sport in the Mediterranean, where the water is warm and clear. In this picture, a scuba diver is getting a close-up look at a fan worm— the long, feathery parts are its gills.

CHAPTER SIX

RESOURCES

Fish and minerals are rich resources drawn from the Mediterranean Sea. The Mediterranean's resources also include the sea itself. With its warm climate, beautiful coastal scenery, and idyllic islands, the sea forms the basis of the region's tourist industry.

Fishing

The Mediterranean has always provided fish and shellfish food for local peoples. Today, about 120 species are caught commercially, including some of the sea's smallest and largest fish—tiny anchovies and big, meaty tuna. Sardines, sprats, and anchovies are fished from surface waters, while flounder, hake, turbot, and bass are caught near the bottom, along with skate, sole, and monkfish. The fish stocks of the Mediterranean are limited by the relative scarcity of nutrients found in these waters. The shallow waters between Sicily and Tunisia provide some of the best fishing grounds, but only 2 percent of the world's total catch is caught in the Mediterranean Sea.

Farming the Sea

Squid and shellfish, such as shrimp and crab, are caught in coastal waters, where **aquaculture** is also important. This practice of rearing fish in enclosed lagoons by the shore dates back to Roman times. Today, mussels are the main

One technique used by Mediterranean mussel farmers is to support the growing mussels in nets wrapped around wooden posts placed in seawater.

A raised landing net surrounded by fishing boats (above) brings tuna to the surface off the coast of Sicily. It took eight fishermen to get this 570-pound (260-kg) tuna into one of the boats (right).

Fishing Techniques

Fishermen use various techniques to net fish in Mediterranean waters. They use mostly small fishing boats instead of the larger vessels seen in the world's oceans. From trawlers, they lower large nets, shaped like giant funnels, to catch fish, such as sole, turbot, hake and sea bass, that dwell near the seabed. The fish swim into the net's wide mouth and get trapped in the narrow, closed end of the funnel. In another method, fishermen set drift nets up to 15 miles (24 km) long at the surface to catch surface-dwelling species, such as sardines. In Sicily, in an annual event called a *mattanza*, fishermen spread nets on the bed of shallow channels to catch tuna as they arrive during migration.

species produced in Mediterranean aquaculture, especially in Italy. Fish farmers also raise mullet, sea bass, and bream in lagoons or in wire cages suspended from boats or buoys.

With many miles of coastal lagoons, aquaculture has the potential to become big business in the Mediterranean Sea. People also harvest non-edible products, such as sponges and red coral, from coastal waters. They use red coral to make jewelry and souvenirs.

Minerals and Energy

The Mediterranean island of Cyprus is named for its copper, *cuprum* in Latin, which has been mined there for five

Energy Sources

Stocks of coal, oil, and natural gas occur on land and underwater in the Mediterranean. Oil is mined offshore in Italy, Libya, Egypt, and Algeria. Test drilling has located oil in other coastal waters and on the bed of the deep sea, but these sources have not yet been exploited. The Mediterranean region is also a center for oil-refining, using crude oil brought from the Persian Gulf via the Suez Canal.

On land, energy from rivers that drain into the Mediterranean is used to generate electricity in the Italian Alps. In Egypt, the Aswan Dam provides power for millions of homes along the Nile. The building of such dams, however, alters coastal and river landscapes. Dams in Egypt have cut the flow of nutrient-rich water into the Mediterranean, causing problems for the local fishing industry.

thousand years. Other metal-bearing ores found in the region include iron, lead, zinc, tin, and bauxite (which yields aluminum). Iron ore and manganese are found on the seabed in areas where volcanoes have been active, including off Italy's southwest coast.

Non-metallic minerals, such as sulfur and potash, are mined in coastal waters off North Africa and Israel. These minerals are used in the chemical industry and to make fertilizers. Salt, an important mineral in everyday life, can be extracted from seawater by allowing it to flood shallow pans on the coast. The water evaporates in the Sun's heat, leaving behind layers of salt.

A thick layer of rock salt, sulfur, and potash covers much of the seabed in deep

Water evaporates, leaving salt to fill these large pans on the Tunisian coast. As the salt dries, it changes color from pink to white.

Tourists and high-rise apartments and hotels crowd the beaches at Valencia on the coast of Spain.

waters away from the coast. These evaporites were deposited in the distant past, when the Mediterranean almost dried up after tectonic plate movement closed the Strait of Gibraltar. At present, there is no economic way of extracting the minerals from the depths, but they are mined wherever the deposits now lie in coastal waters or on land, for example in Sicily.

A Popular Destination

With a mild, sunny climate and attractive scenery, the coasts and islands of the Mediterranean are among the world's most popular vacation destinations. The tourist industry in the Mediterranean dates back to the 1800s, when resorts sprang up on the French and Italian coasts, known as rivieras. Since the mid-1900s, millions of tourists, especially from northern Europe, have made use of cheap flights to visit the region. Today, tourism provides a major source of income for most nations bordering this warm, sunny sea.

As well as enjoying the many beaches, tourists also visit ancient temples, the Pyramids, and other historic buildings in Mediterranean countries. An amazing 30 percent of the world's tourists head for the Mediterranean to vacation each year. Since the 1980s, the number of tourists flocking to Spanish coasts has exceeded the country's own population. Some stretches of coast, such as Spain's Costa del Sol, have become overdeveloped, with mile after mile of hotels, apartments, restaurants, and bars.

CHAPTER SEVEN

ENVIRONMENT AND THE FUTURE

In recent years, the Mediterranean Sea has suffered from overuse of natural resources. Not only tourism, but too much fishing, excessive use of river water, and pollution have all drastically affected the environment. The landlocked nature of the Mediterranean Sea means that pollution builds up rather than escaping or being mixed with cleaner water. In addition, settlements along its coasts are affected by rising sea levels.

Overfishing

Stocks of some Mediterranean fish have dwindled because of **overfishing**. Most fishing boats are small, usually less than 70 feet (20 m) long. The tight mesh of the nets used by local fishermen,

Rising Waters, Sinking City

Venice, Italy, is one of most famous cities on the Mediterranean coast. Full of beautiful buildings and priceless works of art, the old city has water-filled canals instead of streets, and people get around in boats instead of cars. Venice was built on a collection of small islands that are gradually sinking. With sea levels now rising worldwide, the city is frequently flooded. Italians are fighting to save Venice from the rising water with a series of flood barriers. The barriers should be operational some time after 2009, but even they may not be able to protect the threatened city for future generations.

however, traps even small, young fish before they reach breeding age. This is causing fish stocks to plummet. In addition, long drift nets spread at the surface trap all kinds of other sea animals, such as dolphins, whales, and turtles. The dead bodies of these often-rare species, known as "bycatch," are usually just dumped back into the sea.

The numbers of fish that can be caught by fishing fleets are now limited by authorities. At certain times of year, fishing trawlers are banned in the shallow inshore waters where fish breed.

Coastal Habitats

Over the centuries, people have brought many changes to coastal lands around the Mediterranean Sea. These changes have affected coastal wildlife. Scrubby plants and bushes now dominate coastal habitats where trees once stood. In some areas, coastal marshes and mudflats have been drained to create new land for farms, docks, or housing. Wetland species have been badly affected.

Pollution

Pollution has been a serious problem in the Mediterranean since the 1960s. The problem is worst in coastal waters in Spain, France, Italy, Greece, and Israel, where rivers empty waste products from the land into the sea. Chemicals from factories, fertilizers and pesticides from farming, and domestic waste all end up in the Mediterranean Sea. Poisons build up in the bodies of marine animals, entering the food chain and theatening even the largest predators. The sewage and fertilizers cause **algae** in the sea to multiply quickly. The excessive number of algae reduce oxygen levels, which kills fish and other marine life.

In deep waters, pollution comes from waste deliberately dumped at sea and from shipping accidents, such as oil spills. Accidents can cause problems in coastal waters, too. In 1998, for example, the Coto Doñana National Park in Spain was polluted by poisonous waste that leaked from a mine.

Pollution Control

So what is being done to control pollution? Since the 1970s, conservation groups have launched campaigns to make

Untreated sewage pours straight out of a pipe into the Mediterranean Sea, polluting the water and endangering plants and animals.

people more aware of the dangers of pollution, and they have urged governments to take action. In 1976, the United Nations Environmental Program produced an action plan, the Barcelona Convention, aimed at reducing pollution in the Mediterranean Sea from ships and aircraft and from farms, factories, and towns. Seventeen coastal nations signed the plan. In 1995, the same countries signed an agreement to ban the dumping of poisonous waste at sea by 2005.

Endangered Species

Some Mediterranean animals are now so rare that they are in danger of dying out altogether. Endangered species include harbor porpoises and fin whales; both absorb high levels of poisons from their food, and they also get caught in fishing nets. Monk seals are threatened by pollution, fishing, and disturbance to the sheltered coves where they breed.

Green Invasion

"The alga [*Caulerpa taxifolia*] grows everywhere. . . . It grows as well in front of capes swept by storms and currents as on the soft bottoms of sheltered bays, on the polluted mud of harbors as on stretches of bottom with a diverse flora and fauna. Highly toxic . . . it is thus growing unrestrained, covering and then eliminating many plant and animal species. . . . Its control is more difficult every year, and its eradication . . . can now be classed only as a utopian dream. . . . The story of the 'killer alga' has, unfortunately, just begun."

Alexandre Meinesz, Killer Algae, *1999*

On the Greek island of Zakynthos, loggerhead turtles coming ashore to breed are disturbed by the bright lights and noise of hotels.

Conservation Efforts

Conservation projects are now underway to help some of these endangered species. Several Mediterranean nations have passed laws to protect rare species from hunters. Conservation groups are campaigning to prevent people from

The Camargue nature reserve in France stretches over 200,000 acres (86,000 hectares) and is home to wild horses as well as many species of wetland birds.

shooting migrating birds as they fly over Mediterranean islands, such as Malta. The best way of all to help rare species is to protect the habitats where they live, by cleaning up pollution and by setting up marine parks and nature reserves. The Coto Doñana National Park in Spain and the Camargue in France are two such nature reserves along the coast of the Mediterranean Sea.

The Future of the Mediterranean

The Mediterranean Sea faces a major threat in the future, one that is already smothering life in its waters. In 1984, a few square feet of a seaweed named *Caulerpa taxifolia* was observed growing in the Mediterranean, right in front of the building housing the Oceanographic Museum in Monaco. Often used to decorate aquariums, the species is not native to the Mediterranean, and it is toxic to most wildlife there. With few animals to eat it and a strong growth habit, the invasive plant spread and grew to cover 3,700 acres (1,500 ha) of the Mediterranean floor by 1994. By 2004, the invasion had reached many parts of the Mediterranean, covering more than 32,000 acres (13,000 ha).

As it advances, the *Caulerpa taxifolia* smothers other plant species and invertebrate communities, killing them off and depriving fish and other animals of their food in the process. So far, a variety of methods used to fight the "killer alga," as it is known, have failed to stop its spread. If the spread continues at its current rate, the future of Mediterranean ecosystems will be in grave danger.

Global Warming

A climate change identified in recent years is affecting the world's oceans. World temperatures are slowly but steadily rising, in part because of air pollution from the burning of **fossil fuels**. Gases given off when these fuels burn trap the Sun's heat, producing warmer weather. The rising temperatures are warming the oceans, which makes the water expand and so raises sea levels. There are signs that land ice in polar regions may melt into the oceans because of warmer temperatures, and this would dramatically raise sea levels. If the level of the Mediterranean rises by several feet, coastal cities could be flooded. Scientists also believe that global warming will bring more extreme weather to some areas. It could affect the circulation of water in the oceans, making the Gulf Stream, for example, change course. This change would have a dramatic effect on the climate of the Mediterranean and other North Atlantic regions. Many nations around the world, however, are making an effort to address global warming by reducing energy consumption and cutting down on air pollution.

TIME LINE

By 100,000 years ago Modern humans probably inhabit lands around Mediterranean Sea.

About 10,000 years ago People begin farming in eastern Mediterranean.

About 8000 B.C. First towns grow up in eastern Mediterranean.

About 4000–500 B.C. Ancient Egyptian civilization thrives in eastern Mediterranean.

About 3000–1100 B.C. Minoan civilization flourishes on Crete and Santorini.

About 2000–150 B.C. Ancient Greeks develop an advanced culture in eastern Mediterranean.

1650–1645 B.C. Eruption on Santorini causes tidal wave to swamp Minoan cities on Crete.

1200–500 B.C. Phoenicians establish trade and colonies in Mediterranean.

300s B.C. Alexander the Great, according to some historical sources, descends to the Mediterranean seabed in a diving bell.

240–30 B.C. Romans build an empire that stretches the length of the Mediterranean.

A.D. 79 Mount Vesuvius erupts, destroying Roman cities of Pompeii and Herculaneum.

A.D. 324 Emperor Constantine takes over the Byzantine Empire in eastern Mediterranean.

600s Arab Muslims begin to take power in Mediterranean lands.

1100s–1400s Cities of Barcelona, Genoa, Venice, and Constantinople dominate trade in the Mediterranean.

1453 Ottoman Turks take over Constantinople.

1480s–1500s European explorers pioneer new sea routes across large oceans, leading to decline of shipping and trade in the Mediterranean Sea.

1724 Luigi Ferdinando Marsili makes world's first known map of Mediterranean sea floor, charting waters off southern France.

Mid-1800s Steam begins to replace sails as a means of powering ships in Mediterranean.

1869 Suez Canal opens, creating sea route between the Mediterranean, Red Sea, and Indian Ocean.

1943 Jacques Cousteau and Emile Gagnan invent scuba-diving equipment.

1948 State of Israel is proclaimed in Palestine.

1970 Drilling ship *Glomar Challenger* recovers sediments from bed of Mediterranean Sea that help date its formation.

1976 Mediterranean nations sign Barcelona Convention.

1984 *Caulerpa taxifolia* is first observed growing in Mediterranean Sea.

1995 Mediterranean nations pledge to stop dumping of poisonous waste at sea by 2005.

1998 Spillage of waste chemicals from mine pollutes beaches of Coto Doñana, Spain.

2002–2003 Turkey imposes safety regulations on shipping in Bosporus Strait.

2004 *Caulerpa taxifolia* spreads to cover more than 32,000 (13,000 ha) acres of Mediterranean seafloor.

GLOSSARY

abyssal zone ocean below 6,600 feet (2,000 m)

algae tiny, simple plants or plant-like organisms that grow in water or damp places. The singular of *algae* is *alga*.

aquaculture farming of marine species—such as fish, pearl oysters, or mussels—in seawater or inland waters

bathyal zone mid-depths of ocean water between 330–660 feet deep and 6,600 feet deep (100–200 m deep and 2,000 m deep)

buoy floating object anchored in water used to mark a spot or attach nets

buoyant capable of floating or helping something float in water

civilization developed culture and communities of a particular period and place

Cold War (1945–1991) period of hostility between anti-communist and communist countries

colony territory claimed by a nation or area occupied by settlers

condense change from gas into liquid

container large crate—used on ships, trains, and trucks—that combines many smaller pieces of freight into one shipment for efficient loading and unloading by crane

continental drift theory that landmasses are not fixed but slowly drift across Earth's surface because of tectonic plate movement

current regular flow of water in a certain direction

delta land composed of mud and sand deposited around the mouth of a river

echolocation method of detecting prey using sound waves that bounce off solid objects

empire large group of peoples and territories controlled by a powerful nation or group

estuary area of water at a coastline where a river meets the sea or ocean

euphotic zone upper layer of ocean water, usually defined as above 330–660 feet (100–200 m)

evaporation process of change from liquid into gas

evaporite mineral deposit formed on the seabed after seawater evaporates

forge form tool or other object from metal by heating it and hammering it into shape

fossil fuel coal, oil, natural gas, and other fuels formed in the ground from remains of plants or animals

freight cargo transported by sea, air, rail, or road

gyre surface current in an ocean or sea that moves in a clockwise or counterclockwise circle

habitat type of place, such as a mountain or coral reef, where plants and animals live

hull body of a ship. Some vessels have two hulls, joined by a deck or other structure, for stability.

hydrothermal vent hot spring found in volcanically active parts of the ocean floor. Most hydrothermal vents are found on deep ocean ridges, but in the Mediterranean there are shallow vents located near volcanic islands.

isthmus: narrow strip of land connecting two larger landmasses

lagoon shallow area of water near a larger body of water

latitude distance north or south of the equator

longitude distance east or west of the prime meridian

magma molten rock beneath the surface of Earth

mantle part of Earth between the crust and core. It is mostly solid rock, but part of it is molten.

medieval having to do with the Middle Ages, a period of European history between A.D. 500 and A.D. 1500

microwave short electromagnetic, or radio, wave

migration movement from one place to another

mineral natural, non-living substance

mollusk group of animals with thin, sometimes soft shells, including clams, octopus, and snails

navigation use of animal instinct or scientific skills to determine a route or steer a course on a journey

oceanography scientific study of oceans and seas

overfishing catching so many fish that stocks are depleted or species made extinct

peninsula piece of land jutting out into water but connected to mainland

photosynthesis process in which plants use carbon dioxide, hydrogen, and light to produce their food

plankton microscopic plants (phytoplankton) and animals (zooplankton) that float at the surface of oceans and lakes and provide food for many larger animals

promontory high point of land or rock jutting out into surrounding water

radar system that detects and locates objects by bouncing radio waves off them

reconnaissance survey or exploration mission to gain information of military importance

ridge raised area on land or on ocean bottom

salinity level of salt in water

salvage save or recover objects, such as treasure from a shipwreck

satellite vehicle that orbits Earth that can be used to send signals to Earth for communications systems; or any object in space that orbits another, larger object

seamount underwater peak in an ocean or sea

sediment loose particles of rocky material, such as sand or mud

shingle deposit of small rocks, like large gravel, usually found on coastlines

sonar (short for sound navigation and ranging) system that uses sound waves to measure ocean depth and detect and locate underwater objects

sounding measurement of ocean depths

spit long, narrow finger of land stretching out into water

squall sudden, strong wind that lasts for a short period of time

strait water channel that connects two areas of water

subduction zone region where two tectonic plates press together, causing one to subduct, or dive below the other

submersible small underwater craft often used to explore deep parts of the ocean

tanker ship fitted with tanks for carrying liquid

trawler fishing vessel that drags a large net to catch fish

FURTHER RESOURCES

Books

Dudzinski, Kathleen. *Meeting Dolphins*. National Geographic Children's, 2000.

Oleksy, Walter. *Mapping the Seas*. Watts Library—Geography (series). Franklin Watts, 2002.

Rhodes, Mary Jo. *Octopuses and Squids*. Undersea Encounters (series). Children's Press, 2005.

Stefoff, Rebecca. *The Ancient Mediterranean*. World Historical Atlases (series). Benchmark Books, 2004.

Taylor, Leighton. *The Mediterranean Sea*. Life in the Sea (series). Blackbirch Press, 1999.

Vogel, Carole Garbuny. *Human Impact*. The Restless Sea (series). Franklin Watts, 2003.

Woodward, John. *Tidal Zone*. Exploring the Oceans (series). Heinemann, 2004.

Web Sites

Defenders of Wildlife—Marine
www.defenders.org/wildlife/new/marine.html

How NASA Studies Water
kids.earth.nasa.gov/water.htm

Nova/Deep Sea Invasion/PBS
www.pbs.org/wgbh/nova/algae/

Nova Online/Deadly Shadow of Vesuvius
www.pbs.org/wgbh/nova/vesuvius/

Odyssey/Greece/Homepage
www.carlos.emory.edu/ODYSSEY/GREECE/homepg.html

Volcanoes, Earthquakes, Hurricanes, Tornadoes
www.nationalgeographic.com/forcesofnature/interactive/

WWF Habitats Home
www.panda.org/news_facts/education/middle_school/habitats/index.cfm

About the Author

Jen Green worked in publishing for fifteen years. She is now a full-time author and has written more than 150 books for children about natural history, geography, the environment, history, and other topics.

INDEX